THE SCIENCE OF LIFE

ECOSYSTEMS

by Jenny Fretland VanVoorst

Content Consultant
Dr. D'Arcy Meyer-Dombard
Department of Earth and Environmental Sciences
University of Illinois at Chicago

CORE
LIBRARY

Published by ABDO Publishing Company, PO Box 398166, Minneapolis, MN 55439. Copyright © 2014 by Abdo Consulting Group, Inc. International copyrights reserved in all countries. No part of this book may be reproduced in any form without written permission from the publisher. The Core Library™ is a trademark and logo of ABDO Publishing Company.

Printed in the United States of America,
North Mankato, Minnesota
092013
012014
♻ THIS BOOK CONTAINS AT LEAST 10% RECYCLED MATERIALS.

Editor: Arnold Ringstad
Series Designer: Becky Daum

Library of Congress Cataloging-in-Publication Data
Fretland VanVoorst, Jenny, 1972-
  Ecosystems / by Jenny Fretland VanVoorst.
     pages cm. -- (The science of life)
  Includes index.
  ISBN 978-1-62403-159-5
1. Biotic communities--Juvenile literature. I. Title.
  QH541.14.F73 2014
  577.8'2--dc23
                        2013031909

Photo Credits: Galyna Andrushko/Shutterstock Images, cover, 1; Shutterstock Images, 4, 8, 14, 42 (top); Designua/Shutterstock Images, 7; Red Line Editorial, 7, 27; Peshkova/Shutterstock Images, 10; iStockphoto/Thinkstock, 16, 20, 26; Gleb Tarro/Shutterstock Images, 18; Anton Ivanov/Shutterstock Images, 22, 45; Harald Toepfer/Shutterstock Images, 25; Alin Brotea/Shutterstock Images, 30; North Wind Picture Archives, 33; Ungnoi Lookjeab/Shutterstock Images, 35; NASA, 37; Johan Larson/Shutterstock Images, 39; National Park Service, 42 (bottom); Guy J. Sagi/Shutterstock Images, 43 (top); Steve Carroll/Shutterstock Images, 43 (bottom)

CONTENTS

CHAPTER ONE
Introduction to Ecosystems 4

CHAPTER TWO
Food Webs 14

CHAPTER THREE
**The Importance
of Biodiversity** 22

CHAPTER FOUR
Ecosystems Under Threat 30

How Scientists Study Ecosystems 42

Stop and Think 44

Glossary 46

Learn More 47

Index 48

About the Author 48

INTRODUCTION TO ECOSYSTEMS

It is late afternoon on the prairie. The hot summer sun beats down on the earth. A light breeze ruffles the tall grasses. Far above, a hawk soars on the breeze, scanning the ground for its next meal. A prairie dog chatters below, alerting others to the hawk overhead. Bees buzz through the flowering grasses, collecting pollen. Deep underground, worms mix

Prairie dogs are important members of the prairie ecosystem.

the soil as they tunnel through it. An ecosystem is in motion.

Ecosystems are made up of all the organisms living in an area, along with their physical environment. The environment includes the makeup of the soil, the pattern of rainfall, the average temperature, the availability of water, and other factors. Some of these living things and conditions work together to support and sustain one another. Others compete with each other for space and nutrients.

Ecosystems and Biomes

Large groups of ecosystems are called biomes. A biome is defined by the plants and animals adapted to live in that climate. Earth's major biomes include oceans, freshwater lakes and rivers, deserts, grasslands, temperate forests, tropical forests, mountains, and polar regions. Similar biomes can be found across the globe. Brazil and Malaysia are many thousands of miles apart, but they are both home to

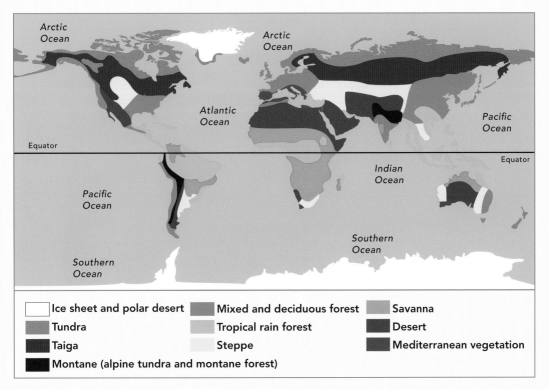

Biomes of the World

This map shows the many biomes that exist on Earth. Which one do you live in? What kind of animals do you find there? How are these animals adapted to live in your biome?

tropical rain forests. The tropical rain forests in both countries contain many similar plants, animals, soils, and climates.

The word *biome* refers to a certain type of environment, while *ecosystem* refers to how all the things in that environment work together. The elements that make up each ecosystem have adapted

Understanding soil makes it possible for people to grow important crops.

to small differences in climate and the environment inside the biome. Ecosystems can be as large as an ocean, but they can also be as small as a puddle.

Parts of an Ecosystem

Scientists who study ecosystems are called ecologists. Ecologists study the individual parts of an ecosystem. They also study how those parts work together. An ecosystem is made up of both nonliving and living parts. Let's look at these parts from the ground up.

At the bottom of many ecosystems is soil. Soil provides plants with the nutrients they need to grow. It also holds them in place and stores the water plants and animals need to survive. Soil is home to many living things, from moles to worms to bacteria.

Water is another key part of ecosystems. When space probes landed on Mars looking for signs of life, what they were really looking for were signs of water. That's because water is absolutely necessary for life. The cells of all living things—from foxes to ferns—need water to function. As much as 60 percent of your body is water.

The Body

Now that you know more about what an ecosystem is, it might not surprise you to learn that your own body is a kind of ecosystem. Made up of bone and tissue, run by organs, fed by blood, and populated with microorganisms, all of the elements of your body work together. If one element of the ecosystem is injured or becomes ill, it affects the entire ecosystem.

The energy that powers nearly all of Earth's ecosystems comes from the sun.

And water is a home for many living things as well, such as fish and dolphins.

Another key part of ecosystems is the atmosphere. The atmosphere is the layer of gases surrounding the planet. It provides oxygen and carbon dioxide for the plants and animals in an ecosystem. Animals breathe in oxygen and breathe out carbon dioxide. Plants take in carbon dioxide and release oxygen. Plants and animals survive by working together.

The heat and light from the sun are an ecosystem's original power source. The sun's light provides energy that lets plants grow.

Habitats

Habitats are areas that contain all the things an organism, such as a plant or animal, needs to survive. Some animals can live in a variety of habitats. For example, wolves live in more places than most other animals. Their habitats are found all over the world. Other animals have specific needs which limit their habitat to specific areas. The saguaro cactus's primary habitat is in the Sonoran Desert of Arizona.

Some animals eat the plants, and some animals eat other animals. Each time something gets eaten, the original energy from the sun moves up the food chain. The sun's heat fuels the water cycle, carrying water into the clouds and dropping it back down as rain.

Ecosystems have lots of different living organisms that interact with each other. They include plants, animals, bacteria, and fungi. The relationships among these organisms are the most dynamic parts of an ecosystem.

National Geographic magazine interviewed ecologist Dr. Zeb Hogan about what a normal day at work is like for him. He talked about the work he is doing studying fish in Southeast Asia:

> *When I am in the field, I spend almost all of my time on or near the water. In Southeast Asia, most of my field sites are near populated areas and I rely on fishers to help gather the information that I need. In Cambodia, I stay in Phnom Penh and usually go to the river twice a day (once in the morning and once in the evening). We own a small boat and take it along the river to meet with as many fishers as possible. If the fishers catch an endangered fish, we work with them to get the fish tagged and released back into the water.*
>
> Source: "Interview with Zeb Hogan, Aquatic Ecologist." *National Geographic Kids,* 2013. Web. Accessed July 31, 2013.

What's the Big Idea?

How does Dr. Hogan's work connect with the definition of an ecosystem? Do you think he considers the local fishers to be a part of the ecosystem he is studying? Pick out details that support your view. What ecosystems might you be a part of?

CHAPTER TWO

FOOD WEBS

An ecosystem is a web of relationships. It makes sense that one of the best ways to understand an ecosystem is by looking at the relationships among its living things. This relationship is called a food web. A food web shows the way energy flows through an ecosystem from one organism to another.

Even tiny mushrooms play key roles in forest ecosystems.

Jungles are made up of many different producers.

Life on Earth is driven by energy. The living things in an ecosystem—plants, animals, bacteria, and fungi—all move energy through the ecosystem. All of them play important roles in the food web. The roles can be divided into three categories: producers, consumers, and decomposers.

Producers

Energy enters many ecosystems from the sun. Light takes about eight minutes to travel from the sun to Earth's surface. There, the leaves of green plants absorb the sunlight. These plants take in energy from the sun, carbon dioxide from the atmosphere, and water from the soil. Using these ingredients, they create sugar and oxygen. This process is called photosynthesis. The sugar helps the plants, including grasses, bushes, trees, and many others, grow tall and strong. These plants are known as producers because they use carbon dioxide, water, and sunlight to produce food energy.

The Dark Sea Floor

One food web that is not driven by solar energy is in the deepest parts of the ocean floor where sunlight never reaches. Here, microorganisms gather around vents in the crust of the earth. The vents pump out hot water filled with a chemical called hydrogen sulfide. Some bacteria use this chemical instead of sunlight as their energy source.

Even carnivores, such as grizzly bears, get their energy from the sun through food webs.

Consumers

Animals called herbivores eat plants. When they do, the plant's energy enters their bodies and fuels their growth. But the energy does not stop there. Herbivores are prey for other animals. Carnivores eat herbivores and use their meat to create energy for themselves. Omnivores eat both meat and plants. All of these animals—herbivores, carnivores, and omnivores—are known as consumers. Their energy originally comes from the sun.

Decomposers

When you have things you don't need anymore, do you try to recycle them? Nature does. When plants and animals die, bacteria and fungi called

Heating with Trash

Can you heat your home with food scraps and garden waste? Some people think so. Decomposers release lots of energy as they break down plant materials. The energy is released in the form of heat. Scientists and inventors are working on ways to capture and use that heat for everyday purposes.

19

Compost piles are filled with decomposers.

decomposers break down the remains and return them to the soil. The chemicals in the bodies make it easier for plants to grow. Now the soil has the nutrients it needs to nurture new plants. The cycle begins again.

Energy is never lost during the cycle. It is simply moved from producer to consumer to decomposer

EXPLORE ONLINE

The focus in Chapter Two is on how food webs let energy flow through ecosystems. The Web site below also deals with food webs. As you know, every source is different. How is the information given in the Web site different from the information in this chapter? What information is the same? How do the two sources present information differently? What can you learn from this Web site?

Energy Flow in Food Webs
www.mycorelibrary.com/ecosystems

and back again. The energy you take in at meals has been recycled time and time again. It may have once helped an oak tree grow strong and tall. It may one day feed a whale or be a bacteria's breakfast.

CHAPTER THREE

THE IMPORTANCE OF BIODIVERSITY

Most ecosystems have an atmosphere, soil, and water. But different ecosystems have different climates. Polar ecosystems are cold, while tropical ones are hot. The amount of water in the ecosystem can also differ. Deserts are dry, while jungles get lots of rain. Ecosystems also have big differences in the organisms that live in them.

Cold polar ecosystems support fewer organisms than tropical ones.

The number of different organisms in an ecosystem is called biodiversity.

The more biodiversity an ecosystem has, the better it can adjust to changes or threats. One reason for this is that ecosystems with many species are more likely to have more than one species that does a certain job. This means that if one species dies out, others can take its place.

Tropical Rain Forests

Some of Earth's most biodiverse ecosystems are in the tropics. These areas circle the planet like a belt. The tropics include the equator and the areas immediately north and south of it. The warm climate and frequent rainfall there create a perfect environment for life to develop and thrive. Millions of different species live

The Amazon tropical rain forest features many different, colorful birds.

Cutting down rain forests hurts the animals that live there.

in the world's tropical rain forests. In fact, although tropical rain forests cover only about 2 percent of the planet, more than half of all species of plants and animals on Earth live there. Approximately 700 bird

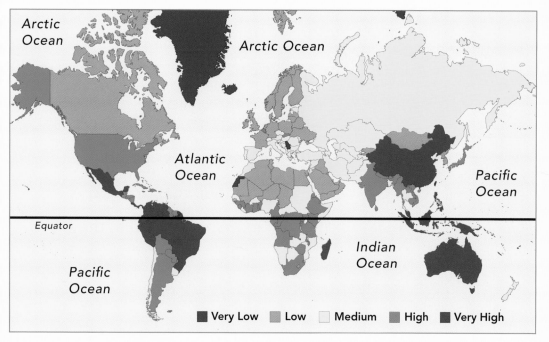

Earth's Biodiversity

This map shows the amount of biodiversity around the world. Biodiversity is often higher in countries near to the equator. Why might this be? What do you think is going on in regions near the equator where biodiversity is low?

species live in North America. But in South America, the Amazon rain forest alone is home to more than 1,300 bird species!

The rain forests of the world are under threat. People are changing the land to transform rain forest ecosystems into farmland. Bit by bit, tropical rain forests are being cut down to clear land to grow crops and raise cattle. An area of tropical rain forest the size of 36 football fields is cut down every minute.

When the rain forest is cut down, plants and animals lose their habitats and die. When they die, they can slow down or stop the energy flow through the ecosystem. This can lead to the deaths of the other organisms in their food web.

Rain Forest Medicine

Rain forest plants provide chemicals for many of today's most successful drugs. According to the US National Cancer Institute, 70 percent of all medicines found to have cancer-fighting properties come from tropical rain forest plants.

FURTHER EVIDENCE

Chapter Three discusses the role biodiversity plays in an ecosystem. What was one of the chapter's main points? What are some pieces of evidence in the chapter that support this main point? Check out the Web site at the link below. Does the information on this Web site support the main point in this chapter? Write a few sentences using new information from the Web site as evidence to support the main point in this chapter.

What Is Biodiversity?
www.mycorelibrary.com/ecosystems

CHAPTER FOUR

ECOSYSTEMS UNDER THREAT

Think of an ecosystem as an orchestra playing a beautiful and unique piece of music. Each part of the ecosystem is its own instrument. Plants and animals may be the loudest, but soil, water, and the atmosphere are also playing. If one part of this ecosystem orchestra is damaged or removed, it changes the music. It may never sound the same as it did before.

Events such as forest fires can damage ecosystems.

Connected Ecosystems

Human activity is threatening many of our ecosystems. Legendary environmentalist John Muir wrote in his journal in 1869 about how everything is connected, even though it may not be obvious. He wrote, "When we try to pick out anything by itself we find that it is bound fast by a thousand invisible cords that cannot be broken, to everything in the universe." In other words, changing or removing something from an ecosystem can have effects that no one could have predicted.

Human activities have threatened to snap these invisible cords, and some ecosystems are beginning to feel the effects. Overfishing, pollution, and invasive species are all problems that face our ecosystems today.

Overfishing

Overfishing can especially be seen in salmon populations. Many people enjoy the taste of salmon and rely on it as an important food source.

John Muir inspired many people to think about their natural environment.

Fishers catch more and more salmon. The salmon cannot reproduce quickly enough to replace the ones caught. This causes their population to shrink. This affects other living things in their ecosystem.

Bears use salmon as a major food source. The smaller the fish population, the less is left for bears. This means bears will have to eat other things, such as berries. The drop in the number of berries then forces other species to adjust. Other animals that eat berries have to find other food sources themselves. Salmon fishing can cause a chain reaction that goes through an entire ecosystem. In some cases, plants or animals may not be able to adapt to the changes. They may go extinct.

Pollution

Pollution is another key problem that affects ecosystems. An example of its effects can be seen in Lake Erie. In the 1960s, the lake's surface was covered with green muck. Many fish were washing up dead on shore. Scientists studied the problem

Human activities release pollution into the air and water.

and found that chemicals in laundry detergent were responsible. These chemicals, called phosphates, went down people's drains with the laundry water.

When the water was released into Lake Erie, the lake algae and plants had a growth explosion. But the bacteria that break down dead algae and plants use oxygen. This removed oxygen from the water, killing fish and other lake animals. Fortunately, this chain reaction could be stopped. Once the cause of the problem was discovered, the government banned the use of phosphates in laundry detergents. Many of the lake's animals were able to recover.

Invasive Species

Invasive species are another threat to ecosystems. Plants and

Climate Change

Climate change can be caused by the release of pollution into the atmosphere. This pollution traps more of the sun's energy in the atmosphere, increasing temperatures. Climate change is a global problem, but it is especially dangerous to polar regions. As the average worldwide temperature increases, polar ice melts. Melting ice shrinks polar bears' habitats and makes it more difficult for them to hunt. Scientists fear these bears may go extinct by 2050 if they are unable to adapt to the changes.

The algae in Lake Erie can be seen from space as cloudy green areas on the water.

animals brought by humans to new ecosystems may have no natural predators. They may crowd out native species. Sometimes these invaders enter an ecosystem by accident. Zebra mussels, for example, hitched a ride into the Great Lakes on European ships. Now they are changing the ecosystem of the Great Lakes by consuming food sources once eaten by other animals. This causes a chain reaction that spreads throughout the food web.

Some invasive species are introduced on purpose. This is usually done in an attempt to solve a problem caused by another species. In the 1930s, Hawaiian

Cane Toads

In 1935, 102 cane toads were brought to Australia from Central and South America. Today, more than 200 million of them live on the continent. The toads have a poison in their bodies that can kill animals that eat them. However, predators in Australia have not evolved a defense against the poison. When animals such as crocodiles and turtles eat the toads, the toxin can kill them.

Cane toads are now considered pests in Australia.

cane toads were released in Australia in an attempt
to control the population of native beetles that ate
valuable sugar crops. But with no natural predators,
the toads quickly became a greater problem than
the beetles.

Earth itself is one huge ecosystem. Every living thing has a place in a gigantic food web. The choices made by human beings can cause major damage to the environment. This damage can ripple across the globe and threaten thousands of species. But people can also make a choice to help preserve nature and keep the ecosystems of Earth alive.

In a 1991 interview, marine biologist and undersea explorer Dr. Sylvia Earle discussed people's responsibility to preserve and protect our planetary ecosystem:

> *We are all together in this. We are all together in this single living ecosystem called planet earth. As we learn how we fit into the greater scheme of things and begin to understand how the system works, we can plan ahead, we can use the resources responsibly, to show some respect for this inheritance that goes back 4.6 billion years. . . . If we are really intelligent, we will learn that we are a part of this system, and not apart from it.*
>
> Source: Sylvia Earle. Interview. *Academy of Achievement*, January 27, 1991. Web. Accessed July 31, 2013.

Consider Your Audience

Review this passage closely. Consider how you would adapt it for a different audience, such as your parents, your principal, or a younger brother or sister. Write a blog post conveying this same information for the new audience. How does your new approach differ from the original text and why?

Studying Soil

Because an ecosystem is made up of many different parts, ecologists use many different tools to study them. For example, ecologists studying the makeup of soil in an area will need digging tools for collecting soil. Sometimes the scientists use drills to dig deep into the earth. Once they have the soil, they use special instruments that measure how much water is in the soil and which chemicals are present.

Studying soil can teach ecologists about how ecosystems work.

Camera Traps

Ecologists often use camera traps to document the behavior of animals in the wild. These cameras are triggered by motion. When an animal enters the frame, the camera begins recording. Ecologists can learn a great deal about the animal without disturbing it. Scientists can then view the footage repeatedly or in slow motion. This helps them study the animal's behavior in detail. It also shows scientists how ecosystems work when they are untouched by people.

Camera traps can show ecologists how shy animals behave when people aren't around.

Tracking Devices

Ecologists can follow animals in their natural habitat using tracking devices. These tags, collars, or chips use radio signals to tell scientists where an animal is and where it has been. This helps ecologists figure out the size of an animal's territory or the times of day when it is most active. This information can help ecologists figure out how different ecosystems interact at different times and places.

Ecologists often put tracking devices in special collars.

Tiny Ecosystems

It can be tough to see changes in huge ecosystems. Some ecologists are using tiny ecosystems as stand-ins for big ones. For example, they study the carnivorous pitcher plant. This plant, which traps insects in its own pool of water, acts a bit like a tiny lake. It has its own little ecosystem of insects and bacteria. If scientists remove the top predator, the fly larvae, from the plant, they can see how the ecosystem reacts without it. They can then make theories about larger ecosystems based on the result.

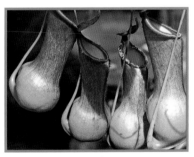

Each pitcher plant is its own tiny ecosystem.

Why Do I Care?

Tasty foods from the tropics, such as bananas, are likely part of your diet no matter where you live. Can you think of a tropical rain forest food that you like to eat? If that food no longer existed, how would that affect your life? Can you think of any other animal whose life would be affected if that food were to disappear from the rain forest? How would that animal adapt? How would you?

Another View

This book had a lot of information about ecosystems. As you know, every source is different. Ask a librarian or another adult to help you find another source about ecosystems. Write a short essay comparing and contrasting the new source's point of view with that of this book. What is the point of view of each book? How are they similar and why? How are they different and why?

You Are There

This book discusses the field of ecology and includes quotes from working ecologists. Imagine you are an ecologist. What kinds of ecosystems are you interested in studying? How would you get started?

Tell the Tale

Chapter Two discusses food webs. A food chain is a single path through a food web. Write a few paragraphs that tell the story of one food chain. Start by choosing a plant. Where does it grow? What eats the plant? What happens to that animal in the food chain? Be sure to set the scene, develop a sequence of events, and offer a conclusion.

GLOSSARY

biodiversity
the number of different species living in an area

biome
a large regional ecosystem

dynamic
full of energy and constantly changing

ecosystem
the living and nonliving parts of the environment that interact with each other

extinct
no longer existing

food web
the whole group of interacting food chains in an ecosystem

habitat
any area where all the needs of a given population of organisms are provided for

invasive species
a species introduced into an ecosystem to which it is not native

microorganism
a living thing too small to see without a microscope

organism
a living thing

photosynthesis
the process by which plants use light energy to make oxygen and sugar

species
groups of living things that can breed with each other

LEARN MORE

Books

De Rothschild, David, ed. *Earth Matters*. New York: DK, 2008.

Gallant, Roy A. *The Wonders of Biodiversity*. New York: Benchmark Books, 2003.

Web Links

To learn more about ecosystems, visit ABDO Publishing Company online at **www.abdopublishing.com**. Web sites about ecosystems are featured on our Book Links page. These links are routinely monitored and updated to provide the most current information available. Visit **www.mycorelibrary.com** for free additional tools for teachers and students.

INDEX

Arctic, 7, 24, 27
atmosphere, 11, 17, 23, 31, 36

biodiversity, 24, 27, 29
biomes, 6–8

carbon dioxide, 11, 17
carnivores, 19, 43
consumers, 16, 19–20

decomposers, 16, 19–20

ecologists, 8, 13, 42, 43, 45
energy, 11–12, 15–17, 19–21, 28, 36

food webs, 15–21, 28, 38, 40, 45
forests, 6, 7

habitats, 11, 28, 36, 43

invasive species, 32, 36–39

Muir, John, 32

nutrients, 6, 9, 20

ocean floor, 17
oceans, 6, 8
omnivores, 19
organisms, 6, 9, 11, 12, 15, 17, 23–24, 28
overfishing, 32–34
oxygen, 11, 17, 36

photosynthesis, 17
pollution, 32, 34–36

precipitation, 6, 12, 23, 24
producers, 16–17, 20–21

rain forests, 7, 24–28, 44

soil, 6–7, 9, 17, 20, 23, 31, 42
sunlight, 17

temperature, 6, 36

water, 6, 9–12, 13, 17, 23, 31, 35–36, 42, 43

ABOUT THE AUTHOR

Jenny Fretland VanVoorst is a writer and editor of books for young people. She enjoys learning about all kinds of topics. She lives in Minneapolis, Minnesota, with her husband, Brian, and their two pets.